THE
Archive Photographs
SERIES
MORECAMBE BAY

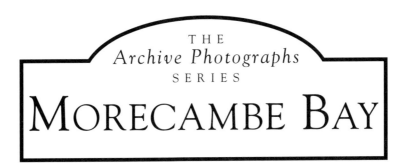

THE
Archive Photographs
SERIES

MORECAMBE BAY

Compiled by
Robert Alston

CHALFORD

First published 1995
Copyright © Robert Alston, 1995

The Chalford Publishing Company
St Mary's Mill, Chalford,
Stroud, Gloucestershire, GL6 8NX

ISBN 0 7524 0163 7

Typesetting and origination by
The Chalford Publishing Company
Printed in Great Britain by
Redwood Books, Trowbridge

Contents

Introduction

The popularity of the seaside holiday for the majority of the northern population coincided with the development of the railway system in the middle of the nineteenth century. Morecambe Bay, with its unrivalled views of the Lakeland hills, soon found favour, first with the workers of Yorkshire, and later with those from Lancashire, as the rail links were extended. Thousands would visit the seaside, either on a day trip or annually, for a week's holiday. The small towns of Poulton-le-Sands, Bare and Torrisholme grew at such a pace that their separate identities were lost, and in 1889 they adopted the name of the bay, 'Morecambe', to describe the enlarged town. The West End had already extended as far as the Heysham boundary. Lodging houses and hotels provided accommodation to meet the growing demand. The Midland was the town's leading hotel, but the King's Arms, the West View Hotel, the Crown, the Queen's, the Royal, the Leeds and the Pier were popular alternatives along the sea front. The Imperial Hotel, Victoria, Black Bull, Station, Pollard's, Birkett's, Morecambe, New Inn and Ship, if not offering a sea view, also provided accommodation.

Morecambe was not slow to provide the facilities expected by its visitors. The Pier opened on 25 March 1869, extending 912 ft into the bay. With a 300 ft transverse platform at its end, it was a popular collecting point for the crowds, either for a stroll during the day, or for those enjoying the dances held in the evening. The landing stage at the end of the Pier was used for boat trips in the bay, and by those boarding steamers destined for Ireland and other Lancashire resorts. The Winter Gardens, long closed, but now with plans for restoration, opened in 1878 as the 'Morecambe Baths, Winter Palace and Aquarium'. The Summer Gardens, with its pavilion, gardens, and an area laid out for sporting activities, drew large crowds. The Gardens closed in 1905 but, eventually,

Regent Park was created from a section of the land. Sea bathing was catered for on the sands near the Midland Hotel, and bathing vans feature on many of the early postcards of the resort.

Although Morecambe was the resort which attracted the majority of visitors, excursions by wagonette revealed the beauty of the area. Many of the smaller villages found favour with the families who returned to the same location year after year.

The industry of the area was inevitably linked to the sea and, initially, Morecambe Harbour was used by the Midland Railway for its voyages to Northern Ireland. Restrictions in sailing times from the Stone Jetty, due to the shallow depth at low water, caused the railway company to contemplate alternatives. Heysham, with its adequate depth of water for sailing, whatever the state of the tide, was selected as the site for the new harbour. Built in four years at the cost of £3,000,000, the harbour opened in 1904. More than 2,000 workers were employed on the project at the height of its construction. The two areas taken over by the workers for housing and other facilities, were known as 'Klondyke' and 'Dawson City', a reminder of the famous gold rush at the time. Local traders were contracted to supply the workforce, and deliveries by hand-cart from Morecambe shops were a familiar sight.

The now obsolete Stone Jetty at Morecambe was taken over by T.W. Ward of Sheffield and used for shipbreaking, at that time the main industry in the town. The local population viewed the arrival of the company as a mixed blessing. Although providing jobs, it was thought that the noise and dirt would deter visitors. The area, however, proved to be a major tourist attraction, and thousands paid to inspect the obsolete liners and warships. The sailing ship *Northampton* was the first to arrive, on 30 September 1905, and ship breaking continued up to 1934, when the yard was cleared to make way for the new swimming stadium. In common with many other seaside resorts, Morecambe declined in popularity after the end of the Second World War. The unpredictable weather and the arrival of the cheap package holiday to the continent combined to defeat the efforts of those providing the attractions previously enjoyed by the British holidaymaker. The decline at Morecambe for many years seemed irreversible but, as the centenary of the granting of its Charter approaches, there are signs of improvements, with the refurbishment of the Stone Jetty. The plans for the restoration of the Winter Gardens will be a further step along the road of restoring the town to its former glory.

One

From Arnside to Hest Bank

ON ARNSIDE SHORE. A Victorian village, Arnside has retained its popularity throughout this century. It was always the destination for families seeking a peaceful holiday.

THE PROMENADE, ARNSIDE. Photographed by James D. Wilson of Arnside, and published in his popular Lilyland Series. Posted in 1916, the postcard reflects the tranquillity of the resort.

3629. Jetty & Viaduct, Arnside.

JETTY AND VIADUCT, ARNSIDE. The Jetty, which replaced an earlier wooden structure, was constructed by Ulverston and Lancaster Railway Co. It was built, following an Act of Parliament, to provide a wharf for sea-bourne traffic. The construction of the viaduct prevented ships from reaching the port of Milnthorpe. The end section was destroyed by storm in 1934, and rebuilt by the London, Midland and Scottish Railway. It was bought by Arnside Council for £100. On 31 January 1983 a storm completely destroyed the causeway. It was rebuilt by public subscription at a cost of £25,000.

THE CATCH OF THE SEASON, ARNSIDE.

12

SEASON.
ARNSIDE.

13

ST JAMES, ARNSIDE. Built in 1866 in the Early English style, the church was enlarged by the addition of another bay in 1884. The East window is a memorial to Thomas Rodick of Ash Meadow, donated by his widow and children in 1880.

ARNSIDE SHORE, photographed by Simcoe and Sons of Kendal, in the summer of 1914. The population at the time totalled just over 1,000. Fifty years earlier Arnside was a little known hamlet.

Along the Dip Road, Arnside.   Lilyland Series   No 62

ALONG THE DIP ROAD, ARNSIDE.

THE FRONT, ARNSIDE. The awning of James Crossfield's grocery store and Post Office can be seen to the right of centre in the photograph. This was at one time the only shop on the promenade. The remaining buildings, in what is now a shopping parade, were at one time private houses. The short stroll from the jetty to the Albion Hotel remains as popular today as it was in the earlier part of this century, when captured by the photographer in the postcard shown below which was published by the Skipton Stationery Co.

CROSSFIELDS' BOAT YARD, ARNSIDE. Crossfield Brothers were renowned for the building of Morecambe Bay shrimpers. Established initially as joiners making barrels, the company were also cabinet makers, upholsterers and pleasure boat proprietors. At one time, their workshops were on Church Road, and George Crossfield lived at Rock Terrace, close by. Three lady artists in the background bear testimony to the attraction of the resort.

ARNSIDE SHORE AND BUSH'S ALBION HOTEL. The Albion Hotel, originally Greenwood House, was built by Robert Bush, a master mariner, in 1821. William James Bush, the licensee in 1913 when this photograph was taken by James D. Wilson, ran a profitable horse carriage business, and advertised posting, carting, furniture removal, wedding parties catered for, and funerals furnished.

ARNSIDE TOWER, a roofless ruin, stands a mile south of the village. Four storeys high, it was a popular viewing platform when this photograph was taken in 1913. Access was by a winding limestone staircase of fifty-four steps.

ON THE KNOT,

ON THE KNOTT, ARNSIDE. Arnside Knott, a limestone escarpment standing some 522 ft above sea level, has been a popular venue throughout this century. It provides magnificent views over Morecambe Bay.

19

ARMSTRONG'S SILVERDALE, offering teas and refreshments when this photograph was taken in 1914. The house at 18 Stankelt Road is now a private residence. The board above the window still remains, though with the name Armstrong painted over.

A VIEW DOWN STANKELT ROAD, SILVERDALE, an unmade road at the time. The population in 1912, when this photograph was taken, was 713. Many of the inhabitants were employed by Northern Quarries Company Ltd.

ST JOHN'S CHURCH, SILVERDALE, built on a site given by Mr Boddington of Manchester, and of The Cove, Silverdale. The memorial stone for the church was laid by Mrs Frazer, wife of the Bishop of Manchester, in September 1884.

COVE LEA, SILVERDALE, the home of Mr Herbert Pennington and Miss Joyce Pennington, photographed in 1910.

Although entitled THE GREEN, SILVERDALE, these cottages, photographed in 1905, are some little way from the area now recognised as The Green. The two large stones, placed strategically on the roof of the nearer cottage, might be thought to be a temporary measure, but they are still in place today some ninety years later.

A general view of SILVERDALE in 1924, on a postcard published by J. Simcoe and Son, Kendal.

FISHERMEN'S COTTAGES, SILVERDALE. The map of the area, dated 1846, shows only the most northerly cottage, which was called 'Bath House'. The other cottages were added in 1868.

BROWNS POINT, SILVERDALE, photographed in 1912. The remains of the old copper smelting mill can be seen in the foreground. Copper mined locally was mixed with tin to produce bronze.

COVE LANE, SILVERDALE. The lane passes through woods to the sea shore and its salt marshes. There are a number of small caves at the shore, the largest being at the Cove. The woods offered protection from the gales coming from the sea, and the village was recommended as a health resort by the medical profession.

FOOT OF COVE LANE, SILVERDALE.

THE ROYAL HOTEL, SILVERDALE, photographed in 1912 by James D. Wilson of Arnside Post Office. The hotel opened in 1904, and the new tenant, when this photograph was taken, was Mr Thomas Charles Greig. He was also a farmer, and in addition to providing stables at the hotel, post horses were available for hire. Solicitors are now installed in the premises at Farnworth House, which was occupied by Cunliffe's, Confectioners.

THE MARSH, SILVERDALE. The sea turf was only infrequently covered by the sea when this photograph was taken early this century, but much of the marsh has been washed away in recent years, leaving a muddy shoreline.

THE OLD POST OFFICE, SILVERDALE, is on the shore road, and is now a private dwelling, Bramble Dene Cottage. The attractive foliage adorning the post office building has now been removed.

SILVERDALE STATION. The rail link between Lancaster and Ulverston was built in 1857. The nature of the terrain was such that the engineers selected a route over Silverdale Moss and Arnside Moss. The disadvantage of this route was that it was some three quarters of a mile from Silverdale village, at its nearest point.

THE NOOK, BOLTON-LE-SANDS. This postcard, posted in 1910, shows a charming group of schoolchildren. Their presence in the road would become increasingly hazardous in later years. A playground for their use was constructed in 1937, a recognition of the danger provided by an increasing volume of traffic. The name board of T. Brighton, house decorator, can be clearly seen on the side of Nook House. The fine building on the left of the photograph is Hawksheads Farm, built in 1665.

CROSS HILL, BOLTON-LE-SANDS, seen from the Nook.

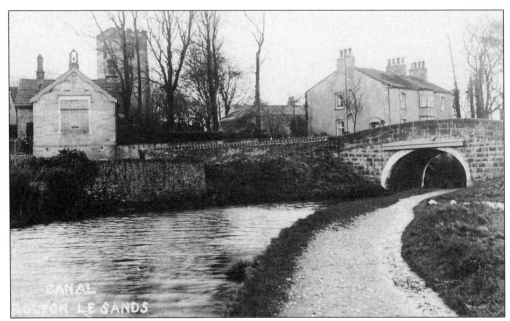

CANAL, BOLTON-LE-SANDS. The photograph is taken from the towpath, looking towards St Michaels Lane. The building on the left is the Old Boys' School, a free grammar school, the rear section of which was built in 1637. St Michaels Cottage is on the right of the photograph.

PACKET BRIDGE, BOLTON-LE-SANDS. The contract for the section of the canal from Tewitfield to Ellel Grange via Bolton-le-Sands was signed on 31 December 1792. Work on the section was completed in 1797. Fishermen's catches were transported to Preston on the canal. Coal from the Lancashire coalfields was transported in barges from the south.

BOLTON-LE-SANDS. The Catholic Church of St Mary of the Angels can be seen on the right of the photograph. Built on a site donated by Miss Coulston, the foundation stone was laid in 1882 by the Cardinal of Westminster. The church was consecrated by the Bishop of Leeds in 1884. The buildings on the left comprise the grocers and confectioners shop of E.M. Bennison, which is now a newsagents. The Black Bull Hotel has a headstone bearing the names of James and Catharine Bibby, dated 1745.

BOLTON-LE-SANDS. This photograph, taken c. 1909 from near Brookfield View, shows two people sauntering along the road which is now the A6 to Carnforth. Traffic conditions today contrast significantly with the scene depicted above.

BOLTON-LE-SANDS, and a view down Packet Hill at the turn of the century. Speight's shop on the left, a draper and hosier selling fancy goods, is now the Packet Bridge fish and chip shop. The attention of the gentleman looking in the shop window is directed to a display of postcards. It is quite likely that the postcard above was available for sale at this shop.

BOLTON-LE-SANDS seen from the Brow.

WHITE HOUSE, HEST BANK, which is now divided into three flats. It was once known as the Old Hall. Prospect Cottage, in the background, was demolished in the 1960s, when a road widening scheme was undertaken. Fish, fruit and vegetables were sold at the cottage. A photograph of Prospect Cottage and the Post Office, which is now Feathers Unisex Salon, is shown on pages 32 and 33. This is the view looking in the direction of Peacock Lane.

PROSPECT COTTAGE AND POST OFFICE, HEST BANK.

ST OFFICE, HEST BANK.

HEST BANK SHORE. A solitary horse-drawn cart makes its way to the beach. The horse and cart ensured rapid transport of cockles and mussels from the sands. They were then despatched by canal to Lancaster market traders. The photograph was taken *c*. 1910.

ON THE GREEN, HEST BANK, always popular as a venue for an outing on a warm spring or summer day. Families would make their way on foot from as far afield as Lancaster and the villages in the Lune Valley. The amount of activity on this photograph taken *c*. 1905, however, indicates some special event on the day.

STATION ROAD, HEST BANK. Prior to the opening of the railway, Hest Bank was on the route across the sands from Lancaster to Ulverston. The journey was fraught with danger, and guides appointed under patent by the Court of the Duchy of Lancaster were based at Hest Bank.

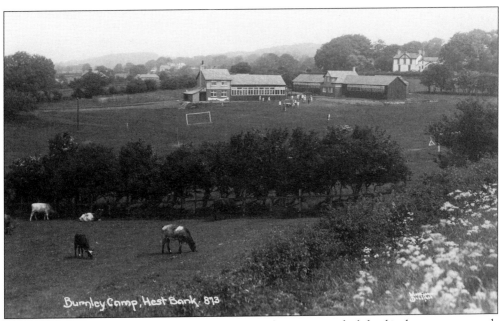

BURNLEY CAMP, HEST BANK. The benefits of an open-air holiday by the sea were much appreciated by the working folk living in the industrial towns of Lancashire and Yorkshire.

HEST BANK STATION.

HEST BANK STATION, located next to the shore on the London and North Western Company's railway from Lancaster to Carlisle, and with a branch to Morecambe, is photographed here at the beginning of the century. It was a popular boarding point in the 1920s, when a grand circular tour from Morecambe to Furness Abbey, Ravenglass and Keswick could be undertaken at a cost of 62 $\frac{1}{2}$ p, including luncheon and dinner. Advertisement hoardings on the platform include 'Sutton Seeds, free by post and rail – no agents', and Crossley Gas and Oil Patent Engines and Plants.

Two

Road and Rail

MIDLAND RAILWAY STATION, MORECAMBE.

MIDLAND RAILWAY STATION, MORECAMBE. The new station building, completed in March 1907, was designed in an Elizabethan Gothic style by Mr W.R. Worthington, the Midland Company's engineer. Mr Wheatley was the architect for the works. The station replaced an earlier one which faced straight down Northumberland Street.

THE STATION INTERIOR, MORECAMBE, built by Messrs C. Murgatroyd and Sons of Idle, Bradford. W.H. Smith and Sons, stationers, occupying a prominent position, carried out a brisk trade with passengers.

THE FIRST TRAIN ARRIVES at the new Midland Station, Morecambe. The first train arrived without any ceremony or official demonstration on the afternoon of Sunday 24 March 1907. A large crowd gathered on the two island platforms completed for the opening of the station. The platforms, each thirty feet wide, were nine hundred feet in length. The one on the north side, seen on the left of the photograph, was covered with a glass awning for two thirds of its length, offering passengers complete protection from inclement weather. Within the bounds of the station proper there was a mile and a half of standing room for trains.

NEW MIDLAND STATION, MORECAMBE. The station building occupied a site between the Midland Railway Company's laundry and the goods shed. The frontage was some 250 ft in length. The exits from the station led into an area some thirty yards from the road, giving ample space for a large number of carriages, as can be seen in the photograph appearing on pages 38 and 39. Along the front of the station was the main entrance hall with three wide doorways in the centre. The vast glass-roofed 'circulating area' measured 174 ft long by 50 ft wide. All the interior walls were in tasteful colours of glazed bricks and tiling. The elevated roof and hanging baskets were much admired by the travelling public.

THE STATION INTERIOR, MORECAMBE. In 1907 there was segregation of the sexes, and of the different classes of travellers. The first class passengers' Waiting Room and the Waiting Room for other passengers can be seen on the right of the photograph. The first class Waiting Room for Ladies, and the Ladies' Waiting Room were on the opposite side of the building. It will be noted, however, from the above postcard, and from the one on page 42, that many intending travellers gathered in the open area.

HEYSHAM PASSENGER STATION photographed early this century. The building was constructed of timber, and the wooden platform is clearly identifiable. Passengers for Belfast, Londonderry and Dublin were required to cross the bridge over the line to the harbour side.

IN LOVING MEMORY: THE LAST TRAM. October 1926 saw the demise of the last horse tramway on the mainland of the British Isles. The last tram was driven by Mr Jack Birch, aged 71, who lived in Lancaster Road. He had driven the first car in May 1887. The last tram was pulled by Adam and Eve, the two oldest horses in the stable. As the car proceeded on its way to Bare, the Mayor, Alderman Gorton, and Alderman Hall, took turns at driving. On the return journey the horses put on an extra spurt, and the speed limit of five miles per hour was exceeded. Several hundred people were assembled at the Battery, where the Mayor made a short speech.

The Bay, Morecambe.

THE BAY, MORECAMBE. The exit from the new Midland Station at Morecambe was directly on to the promenade, where alternative transport was available. Horse-drawn carriages awaited passengers at the station. The alternative option was the dearly loved horse-drawn tram, which can be seen in the foreground. A prominent sign around the open top advertises the delights of the Winter Gardens.

Battery Tram Terminus, Morecambe.

BATTERY TRAM TERMINUS, MORECAMBE. Opened in June 1887, the extent of the tramway run by Morecambe Tramways Company was from the Battery to Central Pier. Fourteen of their cars were sold to Morecambe Corporation in 1909 and car number 16, photographed above, was sold to the Corporation in 1922. The postal date on the card is 6 September 1926, one month before the horse-drawn tram service was to cease.

45

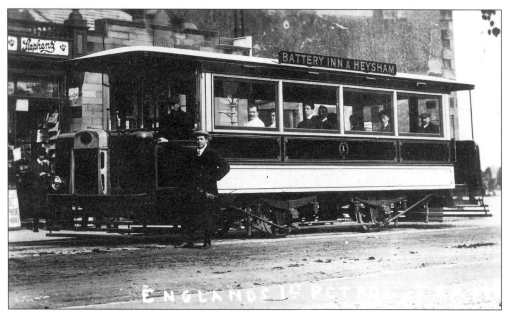

ENGLAND'S FIRST PETROL TRAM. Morecambe Tramways Company had the distinction of operating the first petrol traction vehicles, on a tramway. The cars were all single-deckers and operated over a route of one and a quarter miles from the Battery Inn to Strawberry Gardens, Heysham. The service commenced on 15 January 1912 and the first car carried an invited party. The cars were built by Leyland Motors, and the fleet consisted of four cars, the first three built in 1911, and the fourth, an open car, in 1913.

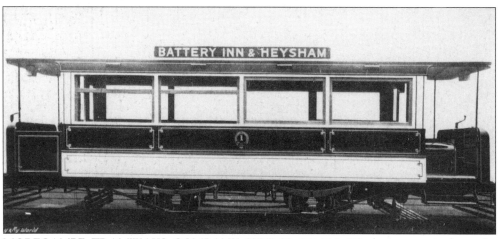

MORECAMBE TRAMWAYS COMPANY PETROL TRAM. Work was required on the permanent way prior to the introduction of the petrol trams, and new rails had to be laid. During the First World War, the cars were converted to run on town gas.

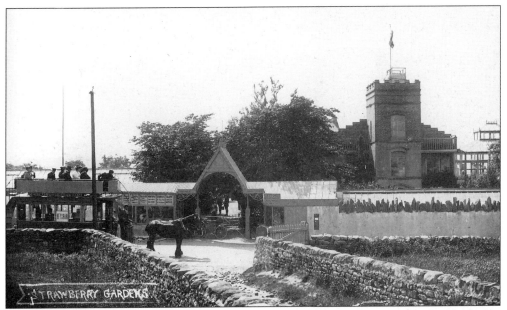

STRAWBERRY GARDENS. A Morecambe Tramways Company open-top double-decker horse tram at Strawberry Gardens, Heysham terminus. The photographer is standing in Sugham Lane. The service opened on 3 June 1887. In 1909 fourteen cars were sold to Morecambe Corporation along with approximately one and a half miles of the route, leaving the Company with three cars operating between Strawberry Gardens and the Battery.

A CHARABANC EXCURSION TO KESWICK. Visitors to Morecambe in the 1920s had the option of either road or rail excursions to the Lake District. The writer of the postcard in 1925 opted for a more staid form of transport: 'I am writing this on a horse waggonette – that is why the writing is so bad. Will be home on Saturday evening, so kill a hen. We have just stopped at Overton to buy some mushrooms – we are on our way to Snatchems.'

A DAY'S OUTING FROM MORECAMBE TO THE LAKE DISTRICT. One of the attractions for visitors to Morecambe was the opportunity to visit the Lake District. A number of coach firms competed for business and after the First World War there were twenty-one companies operating in Morecambe. Councillor Jim Battersby was an early operator, and although his widow sold out to Mr Albert Harrison in 1949 the name Battersby was retained. Battersby took over Silver Grey, founded by Alderman J.W. Carleton, and was operating from the stone jetty in 1962. They also took over Harrison Yates in 1974, and thus created a virtual monopoly. The company closed down at the end of 1979, but within six weeks were taken over by Manx Coach Company Tours. The company was bought back by the Harrison family in 1986.

Three
Morecambe

CHARTER DAY, WEST END, MORECAMBE. Morecambe celebrated its Charter Day on Wednesday 16 July 1902. The first function was the reading of the Charter by the Town Clerk Designate, Mr W. Tilly, at the Council Chamber in Morecambe Street. Reading from a decorated dray, he was accompanied by the Chairman of the Council (Coun. J. Brown JP), Coun. J. Gardner (Vice Chairman), Councillors J.R. Birkett, J. Scott, J. Carleton, J. Kirkham, I.J. Miller, H. Wood, J. Lee, J. Lang, R.B. Abbott, W. Tilly (junior deputy clerk), Dr J.W. Watterson (Medical Officer of Health), Messrs C.A. Brockbank, T. Barrow, J. Bond, W. Clayton, G. Nicholson and others. There followed a two-mile procession through Bare, Torrisholme and Morecambe. It was reported that some 40,000 spectators enjoyed the celebrations, which included an ox roasting and an illuminated water carnival on the Bay.

50

MAIN STREET, TORRISHOLME. The title Morecambe was not given to the townships of Torrisholme, Bare and Poulton-le-Sands until 1889. Torrisholme Post Office and grocery store, run by Peter F. Lomas, has attracted a group of children, no doubt at the photographer's bidding. The tram lines of the Lancaster and District Tramways Co. can be clearly seen, running down the centre of the road. Starting at Stonewell, Lancaster, the double-deck horse-drawn trams made their way via Torrisholme to Morecambe. Three horses were required to haul the trams, built at the Carriage and Wagon Works on Caton Road. Some of the cars were later altered to single-deck open cars.

TORRISHOLME, MORECAMBE. Many of the houses in Torrisholme had whitewashed fronts, and this can be clearly seen in the property on the right hand side of the road. The postcard is dated 20 March 1929, and the writer praises the lovely weather, which has attracted a fair number of visitors, although the season did not start until Easter.

THE ELMS HOTEL, BARE. Originally a private house, The Elms was owned by Mr Thomas Gibson, a Lancaster solicitor. Noted for his generosity, he provided a reading room for the villagers. The hotel was purchased by a group of Yorkshire businessmen in 1934, and re-opened as the New Elms Hotel. In the 1960s, its proud claim was that it was Morecambe's premier residential hotel.

BECK FARM, BARE. Bare beck was formerly a tidal dyke, now culverted, with its outlet to the sea at Thornton Road. The approximate position of the photograph is the junction of Mayfield Drive and Bare Lane.

Bare Hall & Village

BARE HALL AND VILLAGE. Built in 1830, the hall stands on the site of an earlier farmhouse. It was owned by John Lodge and his descendants, who lived there for some 130 years.

A RURAL SCENE, BARE VILLAGE. Photographed in 1910, the building on the right is now Bare Institute. This was the dwelling that Mr Thomas Gibson donated to the village, for use as a reading room.

ARBOUR HOUSE, BARE VILLAGE. Arbour House, with its gable end on Bare Lane, is on the left hand side of this photograph taken in 1913. It was built by John Lodge in 1830, who lived there for a few years before moving to Bare Hall (pictured on page 53).

THE VILLAGE, BARE. The row of cottages on Bare Lane were also built by John Lodge. Arbour House can be seen in the distance. The monkey puzzle tree at the front of the house is alleged to have been planted by John and Ann Lodge.

DOG AND PARTRIDGE, BARE. Set back from the road, the Dog and Partridge replaced an earlier inn of the same name which was demolished in 1900. The lime-washed building on the right of the photograph is the premises of J. Johnson, licensed dealer in coffee and tobacco.

PARK STREET, BARE. C. Finey, photographer of Bare, Morecambe and Malmsbury has recruited local children to give life to the photograph. The traditional hand cart, standing on end, can be seen on the left of the photograph.

BARE PROMENADE. Two vehicles are clearly ignoring the 'No Parking Allowed' sign in this 1930s photograph. It is quite likely that their owners are taking a dip in Bare Pool. The changing room for the pool is immediately behind the shelter on the left.

BARE SWIMMING POOL attracting more spectators than swimmers. Opened in 1906 and built at a cost of £900, it was taken over by the Corporation in 1911.

HAPPY MOUNT PARK, BARE, photographed shortly after its opening in 1927. The writer states, 'The gardens have recently been opened. They are very pretty, and contain an enclosure, with a bandstand for concerts, etc.'

HAPPY MOUNT BAND ENCLOSURE, BARE. An appreciative audience relax in their deck chairs, and listen to the Morecambe Municipal Military Band.

KEIGHLEY VOLUNTEERS, BARE CAMP, 1900. Established in 1886, Bare Camp was a military training ground, where soldiers would spend two weeks during the summer months.

ON PARADE. SECOND WEST YORKSHIRE BATTALION ROYAL FIELD ARTILLERY AT BARE CAMP, 1908.

BARE PROMENADE, MORECAMBE. A party of visitors to the resort is standing outside the Strathmore Hotel in this 1930s photograph. The hotel, with stunning views across the bay, has been extensively refurbished.

CENTRAL MORECAMBE. An indication of the popularity of the resort can be clearly seen on the postcard issued by Matthews of Bradford in the 1930s.

OX ROASTING, MORECAMBE CARNIVAL, 1925. The ox was given jointly by Mr Richard Dugdale and Mr R. Pascoe. It was selected by the Ox Roasting Committee from a herd of bullocks owned by Mr Joseph Towers of Camp House, Hornby. The Mayor, Alderman Hall, is seen carving the ox, and Mr Miller is holding the plate to receive the slices of meat. The roasting commenced at 2 a.m. and lasted eight hours, under the supervision of the official chef, Mr Fred Tyler of Stratford-upon-Avon, who had roasted more than eighty oxen. Tickets with a £5 prize were sold for the weight guessing competition, and eighteen people correctly guessed the weight, which was 12 hundredweights and 1 quarter.

ON THE PROM, MORECAMBE. The clothing worn by the people strolling along the promenade in this 1908 photograph contrasts sharply with the attire of today's generation. The clock tower, presented by John Robert Birkett Esquire JP, Mayor 1903-1906, can be seen in the background.

THE FLAGSTAFF, MORECAMBE. Erected in 1885 by Lieutenant Reid, it had been the foremast of the ill-fated *Put Yona*.

MIDLAND HOTEL AND FAIRGROUND, MORECAMBE. Built in 1847, and formerly called the North Western Hotel, the Midland was undoubtedly the premier hotel in the resort in the last century. Its proximity to the sea and its position near the Midland Railway Station justified this rating. The hotel is in the centre background, and on its left is Fahy's Garage, established in the building which was previously the stables for the hotel. The railway crossing gates in front of the hotel can be identified and the railway wagon, to the left of the signal, bears the name Broughton Quarries Co.

MIDLAND BANDSTAND - MORECAMBE.

THE BANDSTAND, MORECAMBE, a popular venue where visitors could relax after a stroll along the promenade.

BATHING POOL, MORECAMBE. Built in 1935 at the cost of £185,000, it was the largest in the country, catering for 1,200 bathers and, as the photograph indicates, with ample accommodation for spectators. In the 1960s it became evident that extensive remedial work was required. Much debate followed and eventually, in 1975, the pool was closed.

THE NEW MIDLAND HOTEL, built on the site of the former Midland Hotel in 1933. It served as a hospital for the RAF in the Second World War.

EX HMS *NORTHAMPTON* OFF MORECAMBE and approaching the harbour on the morning tide on 30 September 1905.

HMS *NORTHAMPTON AND RALEIGH*, sailing ships moored alongside the stone jetty at Morecambe. They were the first ships to arrive at Morecambe to be broken up by Messrs Thomas Ward.

ORLANDO AND RALEIGH, MORECAMBE HARBOUR. When Heysham Harbour was completed in 1904, Messrs Thomas Ward developed Morecambe Harbour as a shipbreaker's yard. There were many residents who objected to the noise, but the site soon became a major attraction for both residents and visitors. The *Raleigh*, a sailing ship which had been used as a training vessel for officers, arrived on 27 October 1905. The *Orlando* arrived on 17 January 1906. The last vessel to be broken up in 1931 was the *Pegasus*. The harbour site was finally cleared to make way for the new swimming stadium (see page 63). The liner *Majestic* (see overleaf) was dismantled in 1914.

THE SANDS, MORECAMBE, S

THE SANDS, MORECAMBE, showing the *Majestic*.

OWING THE "MAJESTIC". Nº 460.

MORECAMBE ROCKS AND BATHING GROUND. The old Midland Hotel is in the background, on the left of this photograph taken *c.* 1909. The hotel stables and the laundry chimney can be seen to the right of the hotel. Victorian bathing huts can be seen on the beach, in the background. Later they were much in demand with nearby allotment holders, who found they were ideal for storing their gardening equipment.

THE PROMENADE, MORECAMBE. The photograph, taken in 1910, indicates that the horse had not yet been replaced by the motor vehicle. Horse landaus and a horse tram are making their way along the promenade. Motor buses, run by the Corporation, were to arrive in 1918. The picture postcard shop on the right of the photograph is a reminder that postcards were at the height of their popularity. A. Poole, photographer of Northumberland Street, advertises 'A portrait taken in 5 minutes'. Twelve portraits cost one shilling.

HAPPY DAYS, CENTRAL MORECAMBE. Widening of the Central Promenade was completed in June 1930.

CLARENCE STREET, MORECAMBE. Few changes have taken place since this photograph was take, early this century. The newsagents, however, is now a private house.

THE NEW PIER, MORECAMBE, was built in 1868-69, and was 912 ft long. This 1870s drawing shows the original iron structure prior to the building of the Pavilion, which resembled the Taj Mahal. Admission to the Pier was one penny, and a further charge of one penny was made for those who attended the dances in the evening. The landing stage, at the end of the pier, provided access for passengers wishing to reach or leave boats and steamers at any state of the tide.

TECHNICAL SCHOOL, MORECAMBE.
The Art and Technical School was opened on
2 October 1912.

EUSTON ROAD, MORECAMBE. The entrance to the Railway Goods Yard is on the left.
This was the site of the coal depot and also storage for Fyffe's bananas.

WEST END PROMENADE AND ALHAMBRA, MORECAMBE. Built on the site of the West End Market, the Alhambra was opened in 1901 by Mr Norval W. Helme MP. It was built at a cost of £50,000 by Edmondsons, the Morecambe builders.

THE FIGURE EIGHT RAILWAY AND FUN FAIR, MORECAMBE, was opened in 1909 by Mr Helter, who gave his name to the fun-fair ride 'Helter Skelter'. To the right of the castle are the refreshment stand, the skating rink and the amusement arcade.

HAPPY HOURS ON WEST END PIER, MORECAMBE.

LYCEUM'S DEMONSTRATION, MORECAMBE, 2 JUNE 1923. The Spiritualists' Sunday School demonstration was reported to be the largest ever seen in Morecambe. Led by the Morecambe Borough Prize Band, 2,000 children took part in the procession, which marched from the school playground opposite the London and North Western Railway Station, along Main Street, Lord Street, and the Promenade, as far as the Figure Eight Park. John O'Gaunt's Band, from Lancaster, brought up the rear.

Opposite: THE BALCONY, ALHAMBRA BUILDINGS. The photograph of an unidentified lady was taken in September 1909, when West End Congregational Church held a four-day bazaar in the Alhambra Palace. Opened by their pastor, the Revd J. Alfred Buttriss, the bazaar raised £677.

WEST END PIER, MORECAMBE, photographed in 1910, opened in 1896. The pavilion was destroyed by fire in 1915. In 1927 a severe storm broke the pier almost in half.

THE TOWER, MORECAMBE, photographed in 1910, was opened in July 1909. Designed to achieve a height of 232 ft, work was halted when the structure was 154 ft high.

THE WELLINGTON HOTEL, WEST END ROAD, MORECAMBE. The Wellington Hotel and Rigby's store are the main features of this postcard. The Whitehall Picture House, to the left of the hotel, is a reminder of the popularity of the cinema in the period prior to the Second World War.

BANDSTAND AND GARDENS, WEST END, MORECAMBE. The bandstand was opened on 14 May 1910. The popularity of listening to the music was also catered for at bandstands at the old harbour, Happy Mount Park, and on the Central Promenade.

REGENT ROAD, WEST END, MORECAMBE. The West End Flagstaff can be seen in the background. Some of the buildings on the left are: Chapman's confectioners, the vault entrance to the Imperial Hotel, and Dunderdale and Co., grocers. E. Scarth's, Newsagent and Stationer, is on the right hand side of the photograph.

IRVINE TERRACE, WEST END, MORECAMBE. West End Methodist Church, on the right of the photograph, was opened in 1897. It was built on a site given by Mr Richard Crabtree, a local builder.

THE SUMMER GARDENS, MORECAMBE, was opened in 1878 and covered some thirty acres. The gardens were laid out with conservatories, bowling greens, lawn tennis and croquet grounds, ornamental walks, flower beds and terraces. Within the grounds there was also an area for football, cricket and other sports. The Pavilion was large enough to shelter 10,000 people. The majority of the area covering the gardens was sold in 1905 and remained derelict until Regent Park was opened on part of the gardens.

REGENT PARK BOWLING GREENS, MORECAMBE, photographed in the late 1920s, shortly after the park opened.

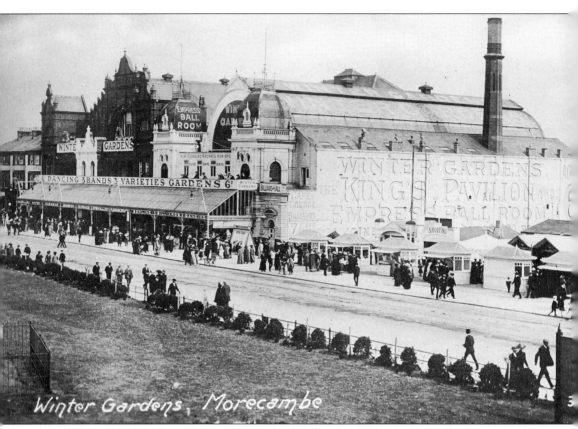

Winter Gardens, Morecambe

WINTER GARDENS, MORECAMBE. The building is in what was described as the Italian style of architecture. It was erected at a cost of £45,000 and was opened in 1878, as the 'Morecambe Baths, Winter Palace, and Aquarium'. The main feature of the building, the domed glass roof, measures 180 ft by 42 ft. The Aquarium, designed under the supervision of Mr W.A. Lloyd of the Crystal Palace Aquarium, consisted of a corridor with twenty six tanks, the largest being 30 ft long. The charge for admission to the Gardens and Aquarium was sixpence. The Baths were entered by a door on the east side, and included a ladies' bath, a gentlemen's bath, and a second-class gentlemen's bath. Bathing costumes were provided. There were also private baths, including salt water, vapour, medicated and shower.

PALACE AND AQUARIUM, MORECAMBE. A drawing of the Winter Palace and Aquarium, *c.* 1880.

THE OLD PIER, MORECAMBE. Every Tuesday and Saturday evening, during the summer months of the 1880s, the steamship *Brier* would sail from Morecambe to Londonderry, calling at Portrush for Giant's Causeway. The return fare was cabin 15s, steerage 6s.

ON THE BEACH, SANDYLANDS, MORECAMBE. The Grosvenor Hotel, on the right of the photograph, was built by Edmondson's of Morecambe in 1899. Boarding houses are on the left of the photograph.

LANGDALE TERRACE, SANDYLANDS, MORECAMBE. A crowd of holiday makers have been persuaded to stand alongside the boarding houses at Sandylands. The Grosvenor Hotel can be seen on the far right of the photograph.

N.P.F.L. Govt. Examiners.

THE GOVERNMENT EXAMINERS, NATIONAL PROJECTILE FACTORY. The photograph is of the Ministry Inspection Department at their picnic, held at Morecambe on 12 May 1917. Their presence in such numbers was due to the visit of King George and Queen Mary to inspect the National Filling Factory on 17 May 1917. Their Majesties were timed to arrive at 4.30 p.m., but long before this crowds took up position from as far away as Cross Hill, right up to the factory gates. Dressed in blue gowns, the girls of the Ministry Inspection Department were in line to meet the Royal Party.

FIRE BRIGADE, NATIONAL PROJECTILE FILLING FACTORY, WHITE LUND, MORECAMBE. On 1 October 1917 a fire started in one of the buildings. Fire and explosions were to last for three days, destroying many of the buildings, and the factory ceased production. People in both Morecambe and Lancaster evacuated their homes, and a stream of people could be seen making for the hills, in the direction of Quernmore. Some Morecambe residents took to the sea. Edward Thompson, who was born in Etruria in Staffordshire, a member of the works fire brigade, is seated on the left of the photograph.

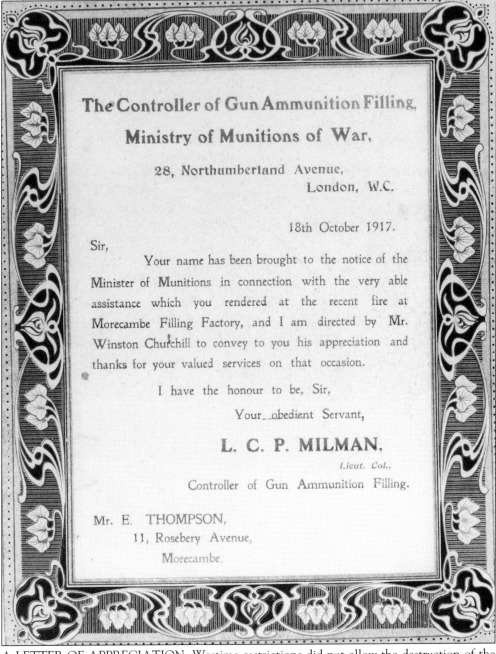

The Controller of Gun Ammunition Filling,

Ministry of Munitions of War,

28, Northumberland Avenue,
London, W.C.

18th October 1917.

Sir,

Your name has been brought to the notice of the Minister of Munitions in connection with the very able assistance which you rendered at the recent fire at Morecambe Filling Factory, and I am directed by Mr. Winston Churchill to convey to you his appreciation and thanks for your valued services on that occasion.

I have the honour to be, Sir,

Your obedient Servant,

L. C. P. MILMAN,

Lieut. Col.,

Controller of Gun Ammunition Filling.

Mr. E. THOMPSON,
11, Rosebery Avenue,
Morecambe.

A LETTER OF APPRECIATION. Wartime restrictions did not allow the destruction of the Filling Factory to be reported fully in the press. Newspapers did carry a report from the Ministry of Munitions that a fire and explosions had taken place at a munitions factory in the north of England. A certificate from the Controller of Gun Ammunition Filling, Lieutenant Colonel L.C.P. Milman, was sent to Mr Edward Thompson, conveying appreciation and thanks for his valued services.

MUNITIONS WORKERS, WHITE LUND, MORECAMBE. The photograph includes Miss Elizabeth Mary (Molly) Newton (second from the left on the back row). When the Filling Factory ceased production in October 1917 many of the workers were transferred to a munitions factory in Hereford. They included Miss Newton and Edward Thompson (featured on page 86). They were married at Hereford on St Valentine's Day 1918, and later returned to make their home at Lancaster.

Four

Morecambe
For Your Entertainment

THE TOWER, MORECAMBE. The ambitious project was to build a tower 232 ft high, and in 1898 the Morecambe Tower Company was formed. The depression following the Boer War caused the Directors of the Company to have second thoughts, and work on the project was discontinued. The tower was demolished at the beginning of the First World War, and the steel used in munitions. The pavilion was capable of holding 5,000 spectators and was a popular venue for shows during the summer season. It was taken over by the Rank organisation in 1952, but suffered the fate of many cinemas when audiences declined. It finally closed at the end of the 1959 season.

MORECAMBE MUNICIPAL MILITARY BAND performing at Happy Mount Park, which opened at Whitsuntide 1927.

THE WAVELETS in 1918 performed at the Harbour Pavilion, reopened under the direction of Charles Howard. The cast is, back row, left to right: Phyllis Ellerton (pianist), Charles Harvard (comedian and entertainer) and Laura Baines (soubrette). Front row: Eva Renee (dancer and monologue artiste), Jack Mavis (light comedian and dancer), Evelyn Dearne (soprano), Mark Cooper (versatile comedian) and Ada Brooks (comedienne and mimic).

THE WAVELETS, MORECAMBE, 1929. The Wavelets, formed in 1914, entertained thousands of visitors to Morecambe. They were the pioneers of costume concert parties, which replaced the old pierrot type. Their first costumes were made by Roland and Riffkins, noted theatrical costumiers of London and Manchester. This 1929 photograph clearly demonstrates a greater sophistication in costume than that worn by the concert party on the previous page.

THE WAVELETS, 1931, launched at Whitsuntide in 1914 by Mr Harry Marsden and his partner, Mr Jess Haigh, who decided to call the company the Wavelets. The alternative name under consideration was The Ripples. Their final season was in 1932, when the party consisted of Charles L. West (producer), Laurie Hallett (pianist), Rex Leslie (baritone), Clarence Pickford (xylophonist and drummer), Tommy Brennan (a well-known revue comedian), Patti Regina ALCM (soprano), Frances Kinders (soubrette), Ivy Bevan (comedienne), and Arabella Allen, a clever Dickens impressionist.

THE WAVELETS, MORECAMBE, 1932.

CLARENCE PICKFORD, XYLOPHONIST AND DRUMMER, is seen here outside the Harbour Pavilion.

THE WAVELETS OUTSIDE THE HARBOUR PAVILION. When the Wavelets first performed in Morecambe, the Pavilion was an open-sided structure with a roof covering built by Mr John Edmondson. Sides were added in 1916, and in 1917 it was enlarged and the sanded floor boarded over. The building was enlarged again in 1919, and seating provided. The building, which attracted thousands of summer visitors, was demolished at the end of the summer season in 1932.

THE VARIETIES, MORECAMBE 1921. Back row, left to right: Mr Billy Malpass (comedian and dancer), Miss Dolle Cecil (a talented entertainer), Mr Will Pfounds (comedian). Front row: Mr Harry V. Newton (pianist and accompanist), Miss Mary Gibson (soprano), Mr Jack Audley (comedian and producer), Miss Lil Marjorie (a dainty soubrette) and Mr Joseph C. Atkinson (baritone).

JACK AUDLEY'S VARIETIES, MORECAMBE, 1926. Back row, left to right: Mr Seymour Scott (funmaker), Miss Bobbie Dallas (soubrette and dancer), Miss Ivy Lawton (contralto), and Mr Tom Leon (pianist). Front row: Jack Hylton (light comedian and dancer), Florrie Butler (comedienne and dancer), Mr Jack Audley (comedian and producer), Miss Winifred Griffiths (soprano) and Mr Pip Dawson (humorist).

JACK AUDLEY'S VARIETIES, MORECAMBE 1924. An admission charge of threepence to the West End Pier was all that was required to attend the popular open air concerts given by Jack Audley's 'Varieties'. The season opened on Monday 24 May 1924, and daily performances were given at 11 a.m., 3 p.m. and 7 p.m. There were nine artistes in the company, but only three survivors from the previous year. Formed in 1920, the Varieties were not only competing with the Wavelets, who performed at the nearby Harbour Pavilion, but also the cinema, where the stars of the screen could be seen at the Winter Gardens, the Tower and the Whitehall.

JACK AUDLEY'S VARIETIES, MORECAMBE, 1929. A photograph by Webber of Queen Street, Morecambe, was a popular method of advertising the forthcoming entertainment.

MORECAMBE'S CARNIVAL KING AND QUEEN, 1928. The opening ceremony of the carnival was heralded by the arrival of the King and Queen, followed by their retinue and a gigantic trades and carnival procession. A week of activity followed, and the carnival ended with a great highland gathering featuring pipers, bands, dancers and sports in Christie Park.

MOBY DICK was built at Glasson Dock, and registered at the Port of Lancaster in 1887 as the *Ryelands*. She was acquired by the film industry, and in 1950 appeared in *Treasure Island*. In 1954 she was purchased by Elstree Pictures Ltd for her part in *Moby Dick*. She returned to Glasson Dock in 1960, and was a popular attraction for visitors to Morecambe. She caught fire in 1970 and was a total wreck within minutes.

DOLPHINS, MARINELAND, MORECAMBE. In 1964 a dolphin pool was opened next to the stone jetty. It proved to be extremely popular in its first year, but attendances dwindled and the Corporation had to come to the assistance of the controlling company.

Five

The Wrath of the Sea

STORM AT MORECAMBE. Inadequate sea defences often resulted in flooding along the promenade. In this photograph a landau and two motor vehicles negotiate the floods near the Figure Eight Park.

GALE AT BARE. Charles Finey, the photographer at Bare, leaves us with a photographic record of the rough sea at Bare at Christmas 1911.

STONE PIER AFTER THE STORM, MORECAMBE. The report of the storm, in March 1907, records the devastation on the old pier. Huge boulders were lifted up, and hurled several yards. The roadway, from near the Midland Hotel to the end of the stone jetty, was blocked with boulders weighing many tons. This report is graphically confirmed in the photograph below.

FLOODED HEN RUNS, MORECAMBE, 24 MARCH 1907.

FLOODED HEN RUNS, AFTER THE STORM, MORECAMBE. After the March 1907 storm an area known locally as 'Capetown' was flooded to a depth of 3 to 4 feet. Scores of fowls were drowned during the night.

FLOODED LANE, MORECAMBE, MARCH 1907. Flooding of low lying land was severe, particularly in the districts of White Lund, Woodhills, Overton and Snatchems. Mr Richard Hodgson, of Anderton Street, lost by drowning fifty ewes and about forty lambs.

THE FLOOD AT CHARLES STREET, MORECAMBE, MARCH 1907. Water stood several feet deep in the houses on Charles Street. Food was taken to the inhabitants by boat, local fishermen acting as pilots. Bread and groceries were handed through the windows, and whenever the occupants wished to leave the area the boatmen obliged. Young people looked upon the whole incident as great fun. Their parents, however, took a rather different view.

AFTER THE STORM, MORECAMBE, 24 MARCH 1907.

OUTER MOSS LANE, MORECAMBE, 24 MARCH 1907. There is little doubt that the inhabitants of these houses were somewhat taken aback after witnessing the scene outside their homes.

THE GREAT FLOOD AT MORECAMBE. The floods penetrated some distance inland. Mr Birkett of White Lund lost fifty of his sheep and lambs.

THE STORM: FRONT TERRACES, SANDYLANDS, MORECAMBE. The storm demolished the front garden walls, sweeping away the stone pillars and iron gateways. The cellars of the houses were flooded, and furniture in the lower rooms was floating about in all directions.

AFTER THE STORM, 24 MARCH 1907. The devastation shown on this photograph records the damage to the workshops of Messrs T.W. Ward. Tons of iron and machinery were displaced.

AFTER THE STORM, 24 MARCH 1907. Huge waves swept over the Old Pier. The old passenger steamer *Ben My Chree*, which had been brought into the harbour for demolition, broke from her moorings and drifted from her position, breaking her bulwarks. The foreman of the works gave orders to his workmen to sink her to prevent her doing any damage.

THE PRINCESS ROYAL —
DAMAGED IN A STORM AT MORECAMBE. FEB. 1913. COPYRIGHT

DAMAGE TO THE *PRINCESS ROYAL* AT MORECAMBE, FEBRUARY 1913. During the storm the yacht *Princess Royal*, owned by the Harbour Sailing Co., broke from its moorings. The boat crashed on the bulking, with the result that one side staved in. When the gale subsided, fishermen assisted to get the yacht on to the Promenade. It was then removed to near Thornton Road, where it remained over Sunday, an additional attraction to spectators walking along the Promenade.

HIGH TIDE AT MORECAMBE. Crowds line the promenade to witness the high tide in 1905.

THE GREAT STORM, MORECAMBE, 1907. It is not difficult to envisage the damage to the Stone Pier, resulting from the gale force winds which produced extraordinary high tides. It was estimated that the tide rose to 29 ft at the height of the greatest storm ever recorded at Morecambe.

THE PROMENADE, WEST END, MORECAMBE. 'AFTER THE STORM'. On many occasions the gardens at the West End suffered storm damage. The low wall surrounding the Green has been completely demolished in this photograph.

WHAT THE STORM DID AT SANDYLAND'S PROMENADE. The scene depicted records the storm at Morecambe on New Years Eve, 31 December 1925.

AMAGE DONE TO PROMENADE SANDYLANDS 1926.

B. S/S. L.B.B.

DAMAGE DONE TO PROMENADE, SANDYLANDS. Early in the evening of 31 December 1925 a gale sprang up, and as midnight approached the wind reached speeds of about 60 miles per hour. Half an hour before high tide 30 ft high waves were breaking over the promenade at West End and Sandylands. The sea scooped out two great holes near Sandylands Church, which are recorded in the above photograph. Huge blocks of concrete were tossed around as though they were corks.

Six

Heysham

THE BATTERY HOTEL. It was from this site that the Volunteers (renamed the Territorial Army after 1904) fired their cannons at targets in the bay. The local population was at some risk during firing, and the steamer *Roses* suffered a direct hit from a cannon ball. Removal of sand and shingle from the area brought danger from the sea, and the Battery site closed in 1884.

HEYSHAM CLIFF PATH. The building on the shoreline was known either as Bay Cottage or South Cottage. Known locally as the Pot House, it was at one time an inn. The field at the rear of the cottage was used as a camp by Boy Scouts; their tents can be seen on the right.

NEW "PETROL" CAR HEYSHAM.
FIRST IN THE KINGDOM

NEW PETROL CAR, HEYSHAM. The Morecambe Tramways Company provided a horse-drawn tram service between Heysham and Morecambe between 1888 and 1912. This route was eventually to be served by the first petrol car in England. The car is seen here, bedecked with flags and bunting, on the first day it went into service on 15 January 1912. Local dignitaries and representatives of other tramways were passengers. The route was served by four of these cars, one of which was open-top. The problem of petrol shortages during the First World War was resolved by converting the cars to run on town gas.

MORECAMBE TRAMWAYS NEW CAR. This 1912 photograph shows the petrol car at the Heysham terminus at Strawberry Gardens. The gardens and tea rooms were popular with summer visitors making their way there early this century.

NEW PROMENADE AND SUNNY SLOPES, HEYSHAM. The sender of this postcard, staying at Heysham Tower in 1928, writes, 'I'm having a glorious time, only its going far too quickly. It's a topping place – beats Blackpool into fits.'

HEYSHAM TOWER. The holiday camp, opened by Mr and Mrs Holden in 1925, provided the accommodation for the young lady writing the postcard. The men slept in tents in the grounds, and women and children in the mansion.

HEYSHAM IN WINTER. Salem Farm is in the foreground of the postcard. The photograph pre-dates 1910, when the farm was extended. The outline of Heysham Church can be seen in the background.

119

THE VILLAGE PUMP, HEYSHAM. The pump, which stood at the bottom of Bailey Lane, was wrecked by a car on 15 July 1930. The little girl on the right of this photograph, taken in 1907, is Miss Kitty Hodgson.

GREECE COTTAGE, HEYSHAM, was at one time the Rectory, and later the village post office. Earlier known as 'Greese Cottage', it is thought that the name might come from the Latin 'grades', for steps.

MAIN STREET, LOWER HEYSHAM. Heysham is famed for its nettle beer, and in particular Granny Hutchinson's, seen here standing on the right clad in her white apron.

MAIN STREET, LOWER HEYSHAM, photographed in 1915 with Mrs W. Kellett's tea room on the far right. Main Street has seen many changes, and the shop on the left is now a private house. The writer of the postcard refers to the child in the photograph as 'a little boy'. Such are the changes in dress over the years!

COSY CORNER HEYSHAM, still on Main Street, with Mrs J. Kellett's tea rooms at No.19. Mrs Kellett can be seen in the doorway of this lovely cottage built in 1633.

THE SQUARE, HEYSHAM. Photographed in 1914, the children are gathered outside Charlesworth's sweet shop. The building in the background is the Lancaster Bank, opened in 1899.

MRS LAYTHAM'S TEA ROOMS, HEYSHAM. Hannah Laytham, who came from Manchester, commenced catering outside her cottage in Heysham using four chairs round her kitchen table. The tea rooms in this photograph were constructed by Mr and Mrs Laytham with the assistance of their children, Ruth, Margaret, Alice and Frank.

HEYSHAM, SHORE ROAD. Pictured here are the stall of Charlie Edmondson, who sold jewellery and shells, and the sweets and ice cream stand of Miss Schofield.

BARROWS LANE, HEYSHAM. Gypsy Smith, palmist and clairvoyant, occupied the building on the left. Landaus owned by Sam Sandham and Bert and Jim Hadath can be seen on the right. Jim Hadath can be seen alongside the rear landau.

HEYSHAM VILLAGE. The village smithy is on the left of this photograph by George Howarth taken in 1906. The barn immediately behind the smithy was the home of Polly Blacow, who could often be seen returning from musselling on the Skeer. She would wash and bag them, and then take them by horse and cart to the Midland Station, Morecambe.

WHITTAM HOUSE FARM, HEYSHAM, photographed *c*. 1914, with a farmer leading a cart loaded with grain. A fixed threshing machine, driven by horses, was housed in one of the barns. The horses were harnessed to a fixed beam by trace leads and were driven round in a circle known as a ginny ring. Farmed by Thomas Pearson, who came to Whittam House from Accrington in 1891, the farm remains in the family today.

ATTIRED FOR A PADDLE IN 1905. HALF MOON BAY, HEYSHAM.

HIGHER HEYSHAM. Berkeley Court flats now stand on the site of the old Methodist Church, the entrance to which can be seen on the left of this 1912 photograph. The building beyond is the old Heysham Smithy.

THE POST OFFICE, HIGHER HEYSHAM, providing Money Orders, Savings Bank, Parcel Post, Telegraph, Insurance and Annuity business. An additional storey has been built on the house, which is now occupied by Frank Casson and his joinery business.

Seven

Heysham Harbour

Heysham Docks 565

THE BUCKET DREDGER CHATHAM at work in Heysham Harbour. Built in 1892 and owned by London and Tilbury Lighterage Contracting and Dredging Company Ltd, she was used by Price and Wills for constructing the harbour. The construction of the harbour was carried out over a period of eight years, and involved exposing about 140 acres at dead low water. The harbour, which was opened in August 1904, was a tidal basin covering some 36 acres, with a depth of 17 ft at low water. The quay walls were over a mile in length, and some 53 ft above the bottom of the harbour. The foundations, in some places, were to a depth of 72 ft below the normal level of the sand.

HEYSHAM HARBOUR, showing the fish quay under construction. The dredger *Preston*, owned by Preston Corporation, is on the left. A Lubecker excavator, manufactured in Germany, can be seen on the right.

DUCHESS OF DEVONSHIRE, HEYSHAM. Built at Barrow-in-Furness in 1897 by Vickers, Sons and Maxim, she was completed in time for the review of the fleet at Spithead by the Prince of Wales (later King Edward VII). She was built for the Barrow Steam Navigation Co., and initially operated on the Barrow–Belfast route. Taken over by the Midland Railway in 1906, she served in the First World War.

SS *ANTRIM*, HEYSHAM HARBOUR. The *Antrim* is photographed here at the opening of Heysham Harbour. She was the first of the Midland Company's new boats to arrive at Heysham. She was 330 ft long, and 42 ft beam, and had a certificate to carry 1,212 passengers, in addition to a large cargo and up to 200 head of cattle. Her average speed was twenty knots, although on her trial run she achieved twenty-two knots. The crew numbered fifty hands. The yacht moored in the harbour is the *Portia*, owned by Colonel Foster of Hornby Castle.

Opposite: SS *THISTLE*, HEYSHAM HARBOUR. The *Thistle* was owned by the Laird line of Glasgow. Completed in 1884 and built by D. and W. Henderson and Co., a Glasgow shipbuilder, she ran between Morecambe and Londonderry and Dublin. She transferred to Heysham when the harbour opened in 1904.

132

S.S. THISTLE
HEYSHAM HARBOUR
JUNO. SERIES 212

Heysham Harbour.

HEYSHAM HARBOUR.

HEYSHAM HARBOUR. Up to 1904 the Midland Railway used Morecambe Harbour for sailings to Ireland. Concerned at the development at Fleetwood, where the Lancashire and Yorkshire, and London and North Western Railways were establishing a joint port, the Midland Railway embarked on an ambitious project to create a harbour at Heysham.

1039 HEYSHAM HARBOUR.

HEYSHAM HARBOUR. This photograph taken in 1904 shows the view from the power station building. Dredgers can be seen in the harbour. South of the power station were cattle lairs, described as clean, comfortable and well ventilated. They were used in bad weather, so that cattle might rest and recover from their sea trip before going on to their destination. Hundreds of acres of pasture land were also available close by. The cattle lairs were directly accessible from the steamers by subways and inclined walkways, which were also linked to the cattle loading pens.

HEYSHAM HARBOUR, photographed by George Howarth of Lancaster in 1904. The bucket dredger *Preston*, with Hopper No. 45 alongside, can be seen in the background at the entrance to the harbour. The bucket dredger *Chatham*, with a dumb hopper alongside, is in the centre of the photograph. Beyond the harbour walls, is a dolphin, installed as a navigational aid prior to the building of the lighthouse at Heysham.

LOADING THE *ANTRIM*, HEYSHAM HARBOUR. Captain Hill, the Master of the *Antrim*, was the senior captain in the Midland Company's fleet. He obtained his Master's Certificate at the early age of 24.

HEYSHAM HARBOUR. The sailing ship in this photograph is the pilot cutter *Albicore*, built in 1904 at Barrow. She was used to take pilots out to the ships before they entered harbour.

TSS *MANXMAN*, seen here arriving at Douglas, Isle of Man, having completed her voyage from Heysham. At one time the fastest steam-turbine steamer in the world, she was sold to the Admiralty, and converted to a sea plane carrier in the First World War. At the end of the war she was taken over by the Isle of Man Steam Packet Company. Used in the evacuation of troops from Dunkirk in the Second World War, she was finally laid to rest in 1949, when she was broken up at Preston.

Opposite: MIDLAND RAILWAY POSTER. The Midland Railway were not slow to advertise their new service to the Isle of Man and Northern Ireland. Leaving Heysham on its inaugural trip, some fifteen minutes after its rival the *Duke of Lancaster* left Fleetwood, the *Antrim* overtook the *Duke*, and arrived at Belfast some thirty minutes before the Fleetwood boat.

HEYSHAM DOCKS. 655/191.

THE *LONDONDERRY* AT HEYSHAM HARBOUR. This postcard, published in the Reliable Series, was available for many years, either as a coloured card or in sepia tones. The *Londonderry* was the first steamship to sail from Heysham when, on 13 August 1904, she sailed under the command of Captain Dunlop to Douglas, Isle of Man. Some 900 passengers took advantage of the excursion, and arrived at Douglas at fourteen minutes past five in the afternoon, the journey having taken a little under three hours. It rained throughout the four hours the passengers spent on the island. Rain continued to fall on the return journey, leaving the exposed upper decks almost empty, as passengers flocked to the lower decks and saloons.

Irish Boat in Heysham Harbour No. 29

IRISH BOAT IN HEYSHAM HARBOUR. The *Duke of Argyll* moored at Heysham some time between 1928 and 1931.

HEYSHAM HARBOUR. 38.

HEYSHAM HARBOUR. This 1906 photograph shows the *Donegal* on the left. The steam coaster on the far right is the *Fisher*, owned by James Fisher and Sons of Barrow-in-Furness.

143

SS WYVERN, HEYSHAM. The *Wyvern* is named after the winged two-legged monster allied to the dragon and the griffin. It is depicted in red on a white background on the Midland Railway house flag.

THE *DONEGAL*, HEYSHAM HARBOUR. The *Donegal* can be seen here, being loaded alongside the South Quay. The quay, one third of a mile long, was built of concrete, capped with great blocks of Shap granite, and faced with timber, extending some ten to twelve feet beyond the concrete wall. The timber fenders were of Karri, from the giant forests of Western Australia.

Eight

The Lune Estuary

DEMPSTER'S, DAISY BANK FARM, MIDDLETON. A delightful rural setting when photographed by Robert Davis of Lancaster early this century. The farm offered accommodation to summer visitors. It no longer exists, swallowed up by ICI and demolished in the 1980s.

THE ROAD TO SUNDERLAND POINT. The house on the far right is the 'Anchorage', built by James Glover Gardner in 1925. Next to it is the boat house, built c. 1920 by Arthur Mansergh, who owned the yacht *Sue*. The Morecambe prawner *Elsie* can be seen in the foreground.

SUNDERLAND POINT, photographed before the road was surfaced in the early 1920s. The house in the background, 'Gravelly', used to be two cottages, one a blacksmiths. The yacht *Peggy*, owned by the Gardner family, can be seen on the left.

AN OLD LANDMARK, SUNDERLAND POINT. The building on the left, the Ship Inn, offered accommodation for those wishing to join in the early nineteenth-century pastime of sea bathing. It was later to become a Temperance Hotel.

147

SUNRISE AND SHADOW, SUNDERLAND POINT. A view of Upsteps Cottage (1 The Lane). It is now derelict, but at one time belonged to the Ship Hotel. The lower half of the building was used for bathing.

SUNDERLAND POINT. Summer visitors can be seen enjoying the peaceful surroundings. Dr Edmundson of Lancaster rented 'Little House' at Sunderland Point, during the summer months.

SECOND TERRACE, SUNDERLAND POINT. Hall Farm, the building on the right, was the Maxwell Arms and popular with summer visitors until it lost its licence. The building with the bay front, further along, was at one time owned by Mr Gibson, a Lancaster solicitor.

THE HALL, SUNDERLAND POINT, at one time the home of Robert Lawson, Quaker merchant of Lancaster. It was from here he would witness ships arriving from the West Indies before they entered the Lune.

SUNDERLAND POINT. Acting on the advice of the Revd A.J. Elsee, the writers of this postcard have visited Sunderland Point in the summer of 1908.

COTTON TREE TERRACE, SUNDERLAND POINT. Although, at first glance, this photograph is identical to the one above, a closer scrutiny shows a later building, Dolphin House, built c. 1914, in the distance.

SUNDERLAND POINT. This postcard, published by Matthews of Bradford, conveys the tranquillity of Sunderland Point as we know it today. In the eighteenth century it was a thriving port, serving Lancaster. Its decline coincided with the building of Glasson Dock on the opposite side of the River Lune in 1787. It later became known as Cape Famine.

A WELL-EARNED REST, SUNDERLAND POINT. Seen from the left are Bert Smith, James (Shirley) Gardner, Tom Spencer, Alderman Turney (from Lancaster), Arthur Townley and Arnold Townley. Dick Bagot is walking along the path facing the camera. William Townley and Tom Gardner are on the right of the photograph. James Gardner, Tom Spencer and Dick Bagot were pilots in the 1920s, and undoubtedly spent many hours awaiting the arrival of boats at the Point.

THE WATER SPLASH, SHALL WE RISK IT? SUNDERLAND POINT,

THE WATER SPLASH, SHALL WE RISK IT? SUNDERLAND POINT. At high tide Sunderland Point is virtually an island, and many unwary travellers have been trapped by the incoming tide. In December 1936 Mr Harold Johnson of Bowerham Road, Lancaster, was driving his lorry over the marshes when the tide surrounded it. He climbed out of his driving cabin and his plight was seen by two river pilots, Mr P. Gardner, and Mr Hubert Townley. They launched a boat and came to his rescue. The gentlemen on the photograph would be fully conversant with the dangers of the incoming tide. The man on the left is Arnold Townley; Bert Smith is facing the camera. Arnold was born on First Terrace, Sunderland Point. He and Bert Smith were neighbours on Second Terrace at the time the photograph was taken. The Townleys' shop on Second Terrace sold cigarettes and minerals. During the summer they provided teas for visitors.

OVERTON VILLAGE.

154

THE SHIP HOTEL, OVERTON. Visitors to Sunderland Point, located at the mouth of the River Lune, would pass through Overton. There they would be able to take refreshments at the Ship Hotel under the watchful eye of Thomas Jackson, the innkeeper.

COCKERHAM, photographed by George Howarth of Lancaster in 1908. Here the story is told of the 'Devil's Stride', from Cockerham Church steeple to Broadfleet Bridge. It was here that the school master outwitted the devil by asking him to make a rope of sand which would stand washing in the River Cocker.

DOCK GATES, GLASSON. The dock, built in 1787, was capable of containing twenty five merchant ships. There was also a graving dock, where vessels were built and repaired.

THE *MORECAMBE QUEEN* AT GLASSON DOCK. The *Morecambe Queen*, an iron steamship, was built in 1872 and owned by the Morecambe Steamboat Co., whose proprietor's were R. Wilson, Robert Birkett, and J. Brown. She was disposed of in 1908.

CANAL TERRACE, GLASSON DOCK. The two postcards on this page are the work of George Howarth, the photographer, of Lancaster. The photographs, taken *c.* 1907, are typical of his work, with the use of children to give an added dimension to his subject. There was no shortage of foreign ships in the dock, and many of the sailors would take the opportunity to send a postcard home. The postcard below was sent by a Norwegian sailor on 26 September 1907.

THURNHAM TERRACE, GLASSON DOCK.

YACHTS IN HARBOUR, GLASSON DOCK. The cargo ship, *Mount Charles*, can be seen moored in the background. Owned by the Lancaster shipping company of Robert Gardner, she was used in coastal waters for some forty years, carrying cargoes of building materials, and also china clay from Cornwall. In spring 1953 she was returning to Lancaster from Parr in Cornwall with a cargo of 300 tons of china clay when she ran into heavy seas. She sprang a leak, and within less than half an hour four feet of water was in the stokehold and the boiler fires were extinguished. Distress signals were answered by the fleet reserve tanker, *Black Ranger*, outward bound from Pembroke. The tanker poured 1,000 gallons of oil on the water, which allowed a boat to be launched and brought under the ship's stern. The crew of the doomed ship were able to jump into the boat and were rescued.

Acknowledgements

I cannot speak too highly of the assistance and encouragement given to me by Doreen and John Read of Heysham. Their knowledge of both Morecambe and Heysham has been made freely available to me in compiling this book. They have also introduced me to people referred to below, who have assisted in providing details for various sections.

I have made extensive use of the records held at Morecambe Reference Library, and have appreciated the valuable cooperation of Lynn Wilman.

A number of people were consulted about the following sections of the book, and I wish to convey my appreciation of the information they were able to offer.
Heysham: Alfred Ernest Bolton, Katherine Gregson, Maureen Walker.
Heysham Harbour: John Pryce, Michael Walker.
The Lune Estuary: Richard Wilton Atkinson.

Thanks must also be accorded to the following for permission to use photographs.
Veronica M. Thompson for photographs which appear on pages 86, 87 and 88.
Brian Pickford for the photographs which appear on page 94.

To my wife Jean Alston, for her involvement in the field work, and for her suggestions with regard to the text.